EURIPIDES

HYPSIPYLE

English translation
by Athan Anagnostopoulos

Based on the reconstruction
and translation of the original
Greek fragments into Modern
Greek by Tasos Roussos

Cover design and ink drawings
by Catherine Kernan

THE GREEK INSTITUTE

EURIPIDES

HYPSIPYLE

This publication has been made possible in part by grants
from the Linda Cabot Black Fund,The Boston Foundation and
The Costas and Mary Maliotis Charitable Foundation.

"...It seems that Euripides combined the myth of *Hypsipyle* with that of *Seven Against Thebes*. Hypsipyle, former queen of Lemnos, is now in exile and a nursemaid in the palace of Lykourgos, King of Nemea. Offering help to the army, when it passed by Nemea, heading towards Thebes, she unknowingly became the cause of the death of Opheltes, the young son of Lykourgos and Eurydike. Hypsipyle is saved from death at the last moment by the intervention of the god and protector of her ancestors and family, Dionysos. In the end, it is declared that the Nemean athletic games will be established in honor of Opheltes, and they will go on through the ages."

- Tasos Roussos

Tasos Roussos, is a noted Greek poet, playwright and translator, who has a profound knowledge and understanding of Euripides' plays. He has translated all of them into modern Greek and many have been performed in the ancient theaters of Epidaurus and Herodes Atticus.

Euripides' *Hypsipyle* is a play with many layers of myth and circumstances, which make it a very interesting piece for the theater. It was well known in antiquity, and had been performed in the ancient theater of Dionysos about 408 BCE. *Hypsipyle* was then lost for many centuries, until a portion of it — over two hundred fragments — was found unexpectedly in Fayum, Egypt in 1906. It had been copied on papyrus in approximately 200 AD. Three hundred lines were complete and enough for a plausible reconstruction.

I must express my gratitude to Clay Morgan for his valuable corrections and Maria Anagnostopoulos, who first produced a successful staged reading of this translation in 2001, with leading Boston actors under the direction of Bill Lacey.

- Athan Anagnostopoulos
Founder and Director
The Greek Institute

CHARACTERS

HYPSIPYLE: A slave and nurse, Queen of Lemnos

EUNEOS and **THOAS**: Hypsipyle's sons

AMPHIARAOS: General of the Argives, and Seer

EURYDIKE: Wife of King Lykourgos

FIRST MESSENGER: Amphiaraos' attendant

SECOND MESSENGER: Argive soldier

LYKOURGOS: King of Nemea

DIONYSOS' CHORUS: Women from Nemea

OPHELTES (ARCHEMOROS): Son of King Lykourgos

SOLDIERS and ATTENDANTS

The English translation of *Hypsipyle* was first presented as a staged reading at the Stuart Street Playhouse, Boston, Massachusetts on December 3, 2001. Produced by Maria Anagnostopoulos for The Greek Institute; directed by William Lacey; stage manager, Henry R. Irving; assistant stage manager, Cheryl Mariolis; with the following cast:

HYPSIPYLE	Paula Plum*
EUNEOS	Peter Clasen
THOAS	Leo Goodman
AMPHIARAOS	William Lacey*
EURYDIKE	Agnes Tsangaridou
FIRST MESSENGER	Richard McElvain*
SECOND MESSENGER	Andrew Dolan*
LYKOURGOS	Diego Arciniegas*
CHORUS	Rena Baskin*
	Nancy Carroll
	Paula Langton*
DIONYSOS	Will Lyman*

Members of Actors Equity Association

HYPSIPYLE

Setting: facade of Lykourgos' palace. Hypsipyle appears holding a baby in her arms.

HYPSIPYLE
Dionysos, who among Parnassos' pines
leaps and dances with the women of Delphi
dressed in deerskin and holding
a thyrsos, it is he who
has sowed my race.
Leaving Naxos, he went to Lemnos
with Ariadne, daughter
of Minos; there he slept with her
and she gave birth to four equally worthy sons:
Staphylos first, then Pepareithos,
who became the king of Skopelos,
third Oinopion, the leader of Chios,
and fourth, Thoas, the master of Lemnos
gave birth to me, Hypsipyle,
his only daughter.
When the time came, my father,
honoring me, let me reign over the island.
I governed justly, but Kypris, goddess Aphrodite,
grew angry with us, the women, because
we neglected a sacrifice.
She punished us with a dreadful curse:
Our husbands couldn't come near us; they went
to Thrace or to the islands and slept with other women.
Our minds darkened with envy —
this, too, was a curse from Aphrodite —
and a murderous rage seized us.
In a secret meeting, we all vowed
to slaughter our husbands —
the Lemnian evil, as it is called!
And one night we killed them, all, in their sleep.
But I couldn't bear to slay
my hopeless father.

I secretly threw him into the sea, in a chest,
for the waves to carry him away and save him.
Then the women became the masters of Lemnos
and I ruled over them.
But one day, a blue-prowed ship, Argo,
appeared on the seashore
bringing the renowned Argonauts.
They cast anchor at the harbor and soon
the island resounded with singing
and the joys of wedding songs.
I chose Jason for my husband; I begot him
twin boys, Euneos and Thoas.
Soon all the other sailors mated
with the island's women. Quickly,
Lemnos became rich with the lovely voices
and laughter of little children.
The women's breasts filled with happiness.
I raised my babies, and dreamed of
a royal destiny for both.
Then the time came for Jason
to leave for Kolchis;
unmoved by my tears
he took to his ship my twin sons,
still babies.
But one disaster brings another.
News came that people had seen my old father
alive; the truth came to light
that I had broken my oath
and had saved him from slaughter.
The women of
Lemnos attacked me,
dethroned me in anger
and planned to kill me.
But I found a way to escape into the open sea;
then pirates caught me
and sold me as a slave
to King Lykourgos, who rules
over this land, Nemea,
along with his wife, Eurydike.
They trusted me to raise their child, Opheltes,
and every day, as I take care of him, I remember

3

my two sons, who, if they are alive now,
will be in the first bloom of their youth.
Are they alive? Are they dead? Who knows!
Yet, in my distress one hope alone
touches my heart — that some day
they will appear here and free me,
unlucky me! I live like a slave,
in sad suffering. My boys! Oh, my children,
come to your mother, I sigh, with eyes
filled with tears! I'll never stop
praying for you to come as my saviors.
This gift, little baby, you offer
to me, your nurse; you remind me,
as you look at me smiling,
of the faces of my own children,
who were taken cruelly from my arms,
and for whom I mourn endlessly.
I am homeless now, with an uncertain fate —
for a slave never has a happy destiny.
Yet a secret yearning sustains me — the hope
that my sons may come here and find me,
guided by their forefather,
divine Dionysos. I do not know
nor have I ever heard whether Jason
found a way to pass through the dark Clashing Rocks,
or whether he returned to his homeland.
If he did, he would have searched to find me, and perhaps
some propitious fate might have led him
here, to me. My baby, let's go inside.
I must feed you; you must be hungry by now.

She enters the palace with the baby in her arms.
From the parodos enter Euneos and Thoas.

EUNEOS
Thoas, look! Look up high and see
the painted pictures on the frieze.
They tell of the deeds of gods
and the passions in myths.

4

THOAS
You're right, Euneos! There at the edge
is Dionysos when he was a baby.
And Zeus, who saves him from the Titans
by putting him into his open thigh; farther down
is the god Dionysos traveling by ship,
holding a thyrsos, and from the mast
are hanging black and red grapes.
At the other end is Herakles,
strangling with his hands the dreadful lion.

EUNEOS
It's surely a royal palace.
You think it proper to go in
and ask for hospitality, or do you think
they'll look at us suspiciously,
as always happens with strangers?

THOAS
We must pursue our goal;
we must find our mother,
if she's still alive, after so many years.

EUNEOS
We were still infants when Jason
took us away from her, and till now,
we've heard nothing about her.

THOAS
No one knows the will of gods;
yet they always grant us hope.
Masters know more
than others. I think
we should knock at this door and we may —
if they welcome us — learn something
of her whom we seek, wandering throughout Greece.

EUNEOS
You're right, my brother. I agree.

(He goes and knocks at the door of the palace.
Hypsipyle opens the door holding the baby in her arms.
She steps forward.)

HYPSIPYLE
Quiet, be quiet, my baby.
Your father will come soon,
bringing you rare, lovely toys
which will calm your uneasiness!
Eh, you! Young men, did you knock at the door?
Blessed be your mother, whoever she may be.
What is it you want here?

THOAS
Excuse us, my lady! We seek shelter
to spend the night.
We've everything we need
and we won't be a burden
to the palace nor will we
touch anything that is yours.

HYPSIPYLE
My master is away from home now,
but he'll be back soon; his queen is inside.

THOAS
Then we'll go elsewhere; when
the master is away,
strangers are not welcome.

HYPSIPYLE
On the contrary; this is a hospitable home;
they always welcome guests.
Since the queen is here,
everything is fine.

THOAS
What land is this? Who governs it?

HYPSIPYLE
This is Nemea; the king
is Lykourgos, Pheris' son, and
his wife
is Eurydike; Opheltes
is the name of the baby I hold.
May I also ask you something?

THOAS
Ask us whatever you wish,
except our names.

HYPSIPYLE
Why should you not say your
names?

THOAS
An oracle forbids it.

HYPSIPYLE
A prophecy from Delphi?

THOAS
A god spoke to us in our sleep.

HYPSIPYLE
The oracle was not from
Apollo?

8

EUNEOS
Dionysos appeared in
our dream.

HYPSIPYLE
Dionysos? Really?
What did he say?

THOAS
To search and find our root.

HYPSIPYLE
Lost long ago or just recently?

EUNEOS
We were still infants when we were lost.

HYPSIPYLE
Are you searching for your father,
your mother or siblings?

THOAS
Family blood; ask no more.

HYPSIPYLE
Do you have a token for recognition?

THOAS
None.

HYPSIPYLE
Hard, very hard task.

THOAS
God and chance will help us.

HYPSIPYLE
I pray that everything turns out well for you.
Find what you yearn for
and return to your mother happily.

Come inside, the servants will take you
to queen Eurydike.
Gladly, she'll offer you hospitality,
following the customs of this land.
May you find what you're seeking.

THOAS
May you be blessed for your good words.

Thoas and Euneos enter the palace.

HYPSIPYLE
Looking into your bright
and calm eyes, my child,
I feel I see light
in a mirror,
and think of how you grow
with lovely songs and caresses.
Listen, a rattling sound
is coming this way.
It's neither the sound of the loom
nor the monotonous shuttle
that made me whisper
the sweet little songs from Lemnos.
I only sing softly
what is fit for babies —
light melodies and lullabies.

CHORUS
Parados
What are you doing in the courtyard, dear one?
Are you sweeping the gate of the palace
or sprinkling the cobblestones with water —
a job for servants?
Or are you singing again of Argo, with the fifty oars,
the song we so often hear from your lips?
Or the golden-haired
sacred fleece guarded
by the sleepless dragon
among the branches of the oak tree?

Or perhaps you remember
the shores of Lemnos where
the thunderous waves of the Aegean sea resound?
Nearby, in a meadow of Nemea,
the whole land gleams with
the bronze armor of the Argive soldiers;
swift-footed Adrastos has gathered
brave warriors
against Thebes, the fortress built
by Amphion's lyre.
Countless shields and spears,
golden arrows and glorious helmets,
horsemen and chariots,
treading heavily
and raising clouds of dust from the earth.

HYPSIPYLE
Ah! I wish I could see the Argo again
coming swiftly with the Thracian wind,
clearing the calm sea,
mooring at the harbor,
and tying the prow ropes;
then Orpheus, seated by the mast
holding his Thracian lyre, resounding
with mournful tunes of Asia.
His song would spur the oarsmen
to draw swiftly their long oars
or to stop again
to catch their breath.
This my soul yearns to see.
Let others sing loudly
of the battles of Danaids.

CHORUS
Long ago I heard from wise men
that Europa, daughter of Phoenike
from Tyros, leaving behind
her city and her paternal
palaces, traveling over the waves,
came to Krete, sacred land of Zeus

where he was cared for by the prudent Kourites;
to the three children she bore
she gave as an inheritance the authority
and power over the land.
I also have heard tales
of another princess, Io of Argos,
who won from love
a hornbearing misfortune,
and lost her homeland.
But for you, our dear,
God will take care
and all will turn out
well and fortunate,
and your father's father,
Dionysos,
will not fail to save you;
he cares for you, and soon
he'll put an end to the ills
that afflict you and your family,
and you'll find again your beloved sons.

HYPSIPYLE
Like an eagle, Zeus snatched away
Aegina, the daughter of Asopos;
he led her to Oenone,
to a calm harbor,
and violated her.
Once, chance led Prokne
and her hunter husband
to a calm harbor where,
mistaking her for a doe, he
killed her unwittingly —
by chance.
Then with mournful songs
he lamented the death she had met.
But for my sufferings,
what lament, what cry, what lyre,
what muse sighing deeply
with tears, will bring
relief to my pain?

CHORUS
First Episode
Oh, Zeus of Nemea, possessor of
this grove, for what reason, I wonder,
do these strangers approach the palace?
They wear Dorian garments. I see them,
coming down from the deserted woods.

Amphiaraos enters with two or three attendants.

AMPHIARAOS
It's terrible to leave your homeland
and, driven by need,
to find only isolated homes and desolate fields,
and no city anywhere.
No one to ask; nowhere to turn.
Such bad luck has struck me.
I am glad, though, I saw
this home in the meadow of Zeus,
here in the land of Nemea.
I'll ask you,
whether you're a slave or not;
to whom does this house belong, oh, stranger?

HYPSIPYLE
To Lykourgos,
chosen in the land of Asopia
to be the priest of Zeus here.

AMPHIARAOS
I need running water to put
in jars, to offer libations
to the gods, that they may grant us a fair journey.
Stagnant waters are not pure
and our army is seized by anxiety.

HYPSIPYLE
Which is your country? Where are you coming from?

AMPHIARAOS
From Mykenae; we're from Argos.

Crossing the borders of our land
we want to make sacrifices first,
so that the gods may guide us
with good fortune to the gates of Thebes.

HYPSIPYLE
What for? May I ask?

AMPHIARAOS
To bring Polyneikes back to his homeland
from which he was exiled.

HYPSIPYLE
Who are you? Who's your father?

AMPHIARAOS
My name is Amphiaraos, I am Oikleas' son.

HYPSIPYLE
Your name and deeds are renowned.

AMPHIARAOS
And you? What are you doing outside the palace?

HYPSIPYLE
I take care of the king's child.

AMPHIARAOS
A relative or a slave?

HYPSIPYLE
A slave, a nurse; not what I was before.

AMPHIARAOS
A spoil of war?

HYPSIPYLE
Pirates caught me and sold me.

AMPHIARAOS
What was a woman doing on the sea?

14

HYPSIPYLE
I fled to save my life.

AMPHIARAOS
Why? For what unholy acts?

HYPSIPYLE
I saved my father, and broke an oath.

AMPHIARAOS
I don't understand you, although I am a seer.

HYPSIPYLE
And that's how dark disaster struck me.

AMPHIARAOS
If you would, tell me your race and name.

HYPSIPYLE
I am Hypsipyle, raised on the island of Lemnos.

AMPHIARAOS
A queen reigning over many women?

HYPSIPYLE
Long ago; now I'm a slave only.

AMPHIARAOS
Before he reached Kolchis, were you not...

HYPSIPYLE
Jason's wife; where is he now?

AMPHIARAOS
At the earth's end; no one knows.

HYPSIPYLE
Alas! For me and my children.

AMPHIARAOS
You had children with him?

HYPSIPYLE
Two sons; if alive, they must be in the prime of their youth.

AMPHIARAOS
They are most surely alive. They will come
and they will find you.

HYPSIPYLE
What did you say? How do you know? Let me hear.

AMPHIARAOS
Your disasters foretell it.

HYPSIPYLE
I don't understand you. Yet, I hope.

AMPHIARAOS
Hope is the gods' gift to humankind.

HYPSIPYLE
With hope I pass my life, in vain.

AMPHIARAOS
Happiness will be sweet in the end.

HYPSIPYLE
You speak in riddles, I don't understand you.

AMPHIARAOS
The gods trap us in oaths.

HYPSIPYLE
I didn't keep an oath, and I am paying.

AMPHIARAOS
Zeus and Necessity decide.

HYPSIPYLE
I did it to save my father.

AMPHIARAOS
An oath will ruin me, too.

HYPSIPYLE
You broke it and you'll pay for it!

AMPHIARAOS
I kept it and this will kill me.

HYPSIPYLE
I don't understand you; explain it to me.

AMPHIARAOS
Death awaits us before Thebes.

HYPSIPYLE
Is there some prophecy? How do you know?

AMPHIARAOS
There is; ask no more.

HYPSIPYLE
Why then go on this expedition?

AMPHIARAOS
Adrastos was persuaded by his two sons-in-law.

HYPSIPYLE
What are Teideas and Polyneikes asking for?

AMPHIARAOS
To take back their kingdoms.

HYPSIPYLE
Will they achieve this by war?

AMPHIARAOS
Yes, by slaughter and fratricide only.

HYPSIPYLE
Why do you go on such an expedition,

17

leading foolish men?

AMPHIARAOS
Against my will; a woman forced me.

HYPSIPYLE
For pious motives or for other reasons?

AMPHIARAOS
By accepting a golden necklace as a gift.

HYPSIPYLE
Who gave it to her? Where did she find it?

AMPHIARAOS
Renowned Kadmos married Harmonia.

HYPSIPYLE
And the gods honored him at his wedding.

AMPHIARAOS
Aphrodite offered Harmonia the necklace.

HYPSIPYLE
The children of the gods are loved by the gods.

AMPHIARAOS
Then Polydoros, Kadmos' son, received it.

HYPSIPYLE
To enjoy the favors of the goddess as well.

AMPHIARAOS
And then Labdakos, who gave it...

HYPSIPYLE
To Laios, his son, and that's how the gift
passed on to ill-fated Oedipus.

AMPHIARAOS
Yes! Polyneikes brought it to Argos.

HYPSIPYLE
Why did he take it away from Thebes?

AMPHIARAOS
To gain what he had in mind:
He offered it to my wife and she
demanded I go to war with them
in spite of a deadly prophecy.

HYPSIPYLE
Will you surrender to an oracle of doom?

AMPHIARAOS
She demands it, and I'll fight.

HYPSIPYLE
Did she accept the gift of her own will?

AMPHIARAOS
Yes! I'll not return from the battle.

HYPSIPYLE
Why offer sacrifices when you know you'll be killed?

AMPHIARAOS
That's the most propitious; no pain
should hinder our piety to the gods.

HYPSIPYLE
Even if it leads us straight to Hades?

AMPHIARAOS
Virtue is loftier than life.

HYPSIPYLE
Oh, noble man, not only in words.

AMPHIARAOS
No one will ever call Amphiaraos a coward.

HYPSIPYLE
They'll think you're a fool.

AMPHIARAOS
Better a fool than a coward.

HYPSIPYLE
All people defend their honor.

AMPHIARAOS
Is it near? The spring with the pure water?

HYPSIPYLE
Very near; near the meadow.

AMPHIARAOS
We don't know the land; will you lead us?

HYPSIPYLE
It's shameful for a woman to wander
outside, in deserted places with strangers.
Find others, they'll lead you there.

AMPHIARAOS
No one is around; the city is far away,
only you can help us.
I must have water for the sacrifice.

HYPSIPYLE
Send soldiers from your army, they'll find
someone to take them to the place you want.

AMPHIARAOS
There will be turmoil when they see
strange warriors roaming through the city.

HYPSIPYLE
Try to find a shepherd or a field worker;
they know where the springs are, and they'll show you.

AMPHIARAOS
When they saw our army crossing
through their land, they hid from fear.

HYPSIPYLE
A woman shouldn't wander outside.

AMPHIARAOS
To assist a pious act, she must.

HYPSIPYLE
My dears, what shall I do? I'm a slave here,
and my duty is to look after Opheltes;
where shall I leave the baby?

CHORUS
You'll decide and act accordingly.

HYPSIPYLE
The spring is not far; I'll take
the baby with me...Follow me
I'll show Acheloos' spring to the Argives.

They leave.

CHORUS
Strophe
Show them the spring, Hypsipyle,
amid the green meadow,
where they may get running water
for their sacrifies so that the Argive army
may have a fair journey,
passing through our peaceful land
without encountering evil or harm,
and reach Thebes,
the fortress with seven gates,
fulfilling the demands of great Zeus.
Polyneikes in full anger
leads them, asking justice
from his brother Eteokles.
And when they end fairly

with the Thebans, they'll head
toward mountainous Kalydon,
and there put fierce Tydeus
on his throne again.

Antistrophe
Exiled both from their homelands,
Thebes and Pleuron,
they wandered about, until
they reached Argos one night
asking for shelter at the court
of Adrastos.
The two exiles, children of brave parents,
engaged in a fierce contest to win a bed for the night.
And the king, watching them
wrestling like wild beasts,
remembered Apollo's oracle:
that he should marry off his two daughters
to a wild boar and to a lion. Then
he flung open the palace gates
and took them both as his sons-in-law.
And then doing them
the favor, he aroused the whole of Argos
and gathered an army
with seven brave leaders.
Now they head toward Thebes
to meet their fate; I pray
that they leave without harming us
as they cross our land.

The Argives have ended their sacrifices;
Hypsipyle appears on the footpath.
She is coming in haste, but she doesn't
hold Opheltes in her arms.
Something bad must have happened;
her face is sad
and tears run down her cheeks.
Soon we'll know; look, she's drawing near.

Hypsipyle enters without Opheltes.

22

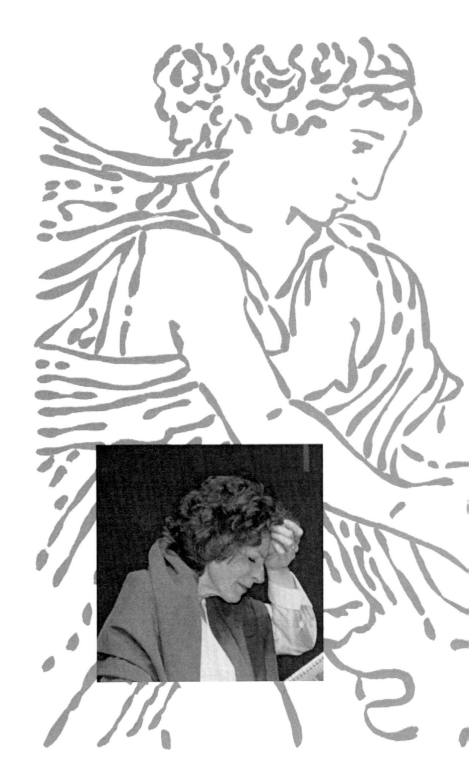

HYPSIPYLE
Oh! Wretched me, wretched me!

CHORUS
What happened, dear?

HYPSIPYLE
Oh! Wretched me, wretched me!

CHORUS
What disaster has struck you? Tell us.

HYPSIPYLE
Alas, alas!

CHORUS
Where's the child? Where do you keep
him?

HYPSIPYLE
He was nearby, not far.
Barely out of my sight! Oh, wretched me!

CHORUS
We're your friends, tell us. Where is he?

HYPSIPYLE
Alas!

CHORUS
Where's the child, where did you leave him?
Why are you here alone?
Did something terrible happen to him?
Answer us! Why do you keep silent?

HYPSIPYLE
Oh, oh, oh, oh!

CHORUS
Laments and cries are useless;
what is done cannot be undone.
Tell us, let us know. Have you
lost Opheltes, the king's child?

HYPSIPYLE
I couldn't find him where I'd left him.

CHORUS
You left the baby? Where did you leave him?

HYPSIPYLE
On the ground, beside a tree.

CHORUS
Alone? You weren't near him?

HYPSIPYLE
I held him in my arms as I led
Amphiaraos to the spring. The child,
frightened by the crowd and the noises,
started crying; I tried, wretched me, to calm him down
as best I could, but in vain.
In the end I put him gently upon the earth.

He calmed down. I left him there and went to the others.
But when I returned right after...
Oh, misfortune, dark misfortune of mine.

CHORUS
What happened? You didn't find Opheltes?

HYPSIPYLE
I left him sitting there,
and he, full of joy, was plucking flowers,
carefree and smiling.

CHORUS
Tell us, tell us, unhappy woman.

HYPSIPYLE
How can I say this, how?

CHORUS
You didn't find the child? You didn't?

HYPSIPYLE
Alas, alas!

CHORUS
What has happened? Tell us.

HYPSIPYLE
I don't know! He was not there anymore.

CHORUS
Oh, disaster, disaster that has struck you.

HYPSIPYLE
I looked around, but the baby wasn't anywhere.
Overcome by fear for him, I ran
through the meadow searching,
and I came to you, my dears.
Has anyone brought back
the child while I've been away?
Ah, empty is my hope, I see it.

You know nothing. Gods, help me!
I pray, that someone will bring the child back alive.

CHORUS
Calm down, don't tremble, they'll find him.

HYPSIPYLE
Too much time has gone by. He's gone, he's lost.

CHORUS
Why are you saying that? You never know.

HYPSIPYLE
Fear for him is strangling me.

CHORUS
Think of no evil. Someone will find
the child and he'll bring him back.
Some shepherd or farmer.

HYPSIPYLE
Then where is he? Why is he not here?

CHORUS
You'll see, he'll come holding the baby.

HYPSIPYLE
You comfort me with vain hopes.
Someone took the baby to keep him
for his own: someone childless, or some
wild beast, finding him alone, tore him to pieces.
My friends, what shall I do now?
I am at the height of ruin.
It's over. I'm lost now. I can never be saved.

CHORUS
You have no word of hope for your friends?

HYPSIPYLE
I fear what's in store for me for the loss of the child.

CHORUS
Unlucky woman, you know well what disaster means.

HYPSIPYLE
I shall leave the palace quickly.

CHORUS
Where will you go? What city will take you?

HYPSIPYLE
My feet and my fear will decide.

CHORUS
Fortresses guard the country on all sides.

HYPSIPYLE
You are right. Yet I must leave.

CHORUS
Think, we're your friends and advisors.

HYPSIPYLE
Someone must help me escape!

CHORUS
No one will help a slave.

HYPSIPYLE
But God will help the innocent!

CHORUS
Gods are indifferent to our misery.

HYPSIPYLE
Then I'm surely lost.

CHORUS
Go to our queen and beg her.

HYPSIPYLE
She won't listen to a miserable slave.
Ah! I wish I could sprout wings and fly away!

CHORUS
This despair is not becoming to you!

HYPSIPYLE
But Opheltes is lost!

CHORUS
Only Fortune will decide that.

HYPSIPYLE
I know my fortune now.

CHORUS
Look! An Argive
approaches, followed by men
with sad faces.

FIRST MESSENGER
Women of Nemea, where's
the master of the palace? Raise the bars
and open the door; I bring news
for him and he must hear.
But first, take this slave inside,
the baby's nurse; she must not stand out here,
for she left the child alone, foolish as she is.

EURYDIKE
Coming out of the palace
Who is the stranger? What does he want,
shouting before the palace?

CHORUS
He's from the army of the Argives; he brings news,
my lady, for your husband Lykourgos.

29

EURYDIKE
He's not here. I am master until his return.
Speak, stranger. Tell me the news.

FIRST MESSENGER
At the meadow's edge, your son Opheltes
died, bitten by a snake.

EURYDIKE
Oh, dark misery, if you tell the truth.
How could my child be there?

FIRST MESSENGER
The slave you have as your nurse took him there...

EURYDIKE
What for? Tell me! Let me hear!

FIRST MESSENGER
We started out here, and crossing
the meadow, we took the footpath
that goes uphill and leads straight
to the small rocky cave
with the pure, rich, gushing spring.
Shortly before we could get there, the infant
started to cry loudly and, after calming him down,
Hypsipyle put the baby on the ground,
alone, without a guard near him.
But the land, at this time of the year, awakens
its snakes in cracks and rocks;
and as the sun's rays warm them,
they come out of their nests.
They absorb the sunlight. Their green,
carmine, blue colors gleam,
revealing the thirst for life
that swells in them and bursts forth
full of wrath and force. In winter,
they sink in darkness and sleep as in death
under Persephone's apron.

We reached the spring and before
we began filling up the jugs with water,
our general stopped and ordered
holy silence, and said
this prayer: "O Zeus, and you other gods
that protect us, bless us that we may fare well
in our far-off expedition.
Change the omens, and let the way
reveal propitious signs to the Argives."
Then, with a saddened face,
he poured libations to the earth and sighed.
When he had finished, he ordered the woman
to fill the first jug herself.
As she eagerly obeyed,
I saw him suddenly stand still, astonished,
eyes blurred in the empty air,
as if he had seen something horrible;
he rushed from the cave; I ran
behind him, too, for I'm his attendant.
I didn't understand the reason for his haste;
what could force the seer to abandon the spring?
It soon became clear. The cries
and shouts of our small companion,
as we proceeded, had awakened a snake
in its nest at the spring.
Aroused by the noises,
the snake slid downhill fiercely,
staring wildly about, shaking
its glittering crest.
Some shepherds further down
saw it and cowered, struck with terror,
unable to do anything. The snake, though,
slid along the footpath's edge
and, as if led by some god,
headed directly toward the baby.
It stopped, raised high
its spotted neck, looked about
with a lethal glance, and seeing the baby
close by, smoothly slithered near him,
fiercely shaking its forked tongue.
But the child sat carefree

on the ground, playing with the flowers,
unaware of any danger.
The snake raised its head over him,
hissing hideously. Some soldiers
saw it in the meadow and
shot their arrows, but they missed.
Then Amphiaraos rushed alone from the spring, approached it,
and shot his arrows through its neck.
The serpent rolled over, writhing,
and slowly stiffened in death.
Quickly, we all ran there hoping for the child.
But in vain; the snake had already bitten him,
and instantly the dreadful venom
had killed the poor boy. With great grief,
our general took him in his arms
and gave orders to take care of the dead baby.
The soldiers took the lifeless body, laid it
gently in a precious wooden chest,
and our leader sends it here to you, to mourn him.

Now let your rightful anger burst
upon her, Queen, that woman who's the culprit,
who didn't give a thought to the fact
that an infant
left alone in a desolate place
is always exposed to great danger.
I have said what I had to say.

He leaves.

HYPSIPYLE
Oh, misery! Oh, misery!

EURYDIKE
Approaching the casket
My child, my child,
my little boy,
you've gone down to Hades
and left me alone,
lamenting my misery.

EURYDIKE
What treacherous fate,
what evil demon stole the light from your eyes
and made my arms orphans.
Untrained, your tiny soul
shall wander now alone
in Hades' dark land,
helpless, guideless.

CHORUS
Great is your pain,
heavy is your mourning,
our unhappy queen.

EURYDIKE
Mourn with me that
the many tears and laments
may bring him peace.
My baby, my offspring,
respite of my old age,
shield of our homeland,
protector of the palace.

CHORUS
Venom, dark venom,
a yellow dragon-snake
stole away your innocent life.

EURYDIKE
You'd be the best youth
in the land of Nemea,
her pride, and in all parts
of Apia the envied prize.

CHORUS
Unjust, unjust is this loss,
uncalled for, inexplicable.
Oh, misery, misery.

EURYDIKE
My baby left unguarded,
alone, there, on the ground,
no one was near you,
to protect your life;
woe, oh, woe unto me.

CHORUS
An envious demon,
a treacherous fate
stole Opheltes from you;
woe, oh, woe.

EURYDIKE
My child, my treasure,
flower of my breasts,
your father will come,
bringing you new toys.
Full of joy, he'll ask for you,
to give them to you, to play.

And instead of your joyful
laughter and lovely sounds,
he'll find your lifeless, tiny body.

CHORUS
A treacherous fate,
a blind, evil fate,
snatched your child away.

EURYDIKE
What did I do wrong, oh, gods!
that you stole away
my life's seed?

CHORUS
Neither god nor mortal
is to blame for his death.

EURYDIKE
The culprit is here, full of insolence.

CHORUS
What do you mean, my lady? Who? Among us?

EURYDIKE
This slave I've kept for my nurse.
She has killed my child.

CHORUS
No, my queen, she weeps! She suffers!

EURYDIKE
Alien, purchased slave woman,
whose tears flow easily at every need,
you'll pay for my son's loss
with your own death.
Mark this:
You won't escape justice.

CHORUS
Answer, Hypsipyle, don't keep silent.

EURYDIKE
Whatever she says is a lie.

HYPSIPYLE
My queen, anger and sorrow
darken your mind and so you think
I'm the cause of your child's death.
But I've loved him no less than you.

EURYDIKE
Thoughtless woman, you have the audacity
to speak to me about good judgment?
Hear your faults one by one.
You left the palace with the child
without telling where you were going,
without getting permission from me, as you had to.
You went with soldiers from a foreign land,
alone, with an infant in your arms,
to a desolate place. Are these sound acts?
Besides, you could have, even before
reaching the spring, pointed out to the soldiers where
the water was, and come right back.
But you put my son down — alone —
and followed the stranger;
and, as if this were not enough — you lingered,
filling up the jug — instead of returning
to the baby's side instantly. One stupidity
after another brought disaster.
You'll find no compassion in me.
I'll punish you as you deserve.

CHORUS
She spoke fairly, now it's your turn
to rightly defend yourself, Hypsipyle.

HYPSIPYLE
A pious and virtuous man
came to the palace; he asked
for running water to offer libations
to the gods for his army's sake; he was an Argive;
his name is Amphiaraos, a seer.

Without any fear, holding
the infant in my arms, I led him
towards the spring; but as we drew nearer,
the child, frightened
by the shouting and clashing of armor,
began crying and twisting in my arms.
I tried hard to calm him as best as I could.
Finally, I put him down on the grass;
at once, as if by a miracle, he stopped crying,
and smiling, he started playing with the earth.
I left him there and went quickly to guide the soldiers.
I came right back; the infant
had vanished; you know all the rest.

EURYDIKE
You yourself admit the wrong-doing
that brought my only son to death.

HYPSIPYLE
I wished no wrong.

EURYDIKE
You ought to have asked me before leaving.

HYPSIPYLE
I had to help perform the sacred rituals.

EURYDIKE
By leaving my Opheltes alone?

HYPSIPYLE
Crying hinders sacrifices.

EURYDIKE
You had the child and you lost him.

HYPSIPYLE
I didn't lose him, fate snatched him away from me.

EURYDIKE
Such fate will snatch you away, too.

HYPSIPYLE
Oh, miserable me, if I guess rightly.

EURYDIKE
You do! Bind up her hands!

HYPSIPYLE
Oh, Dionysos! Oh, gods! Help me!

EURYDIKE
No one helps culprits.

HYPSIPYLE
You are determined to put me to death?

EURYDIKE
You'll pay as you deserve.

HYPSIPYLE
Putting aside anger, one judges more wisely.

EURYDIKE
Not anger but grief makes me shudder.

HYPSIPYLE
You're a woman, and you know
how deeply a woman feels; don't judge me now
when grief and anger strangle you.
A mortal's actions must always be guided by his mind;
reason must govern us.
Wisdom and thoughtful speech set humans
apart from animals.
I'm not the cause of dear Opheltes' death,
although it may appear so.
Destiny led things along a hidden path.

CHORUS
You spoke with courage and skill;
I pray we're counted among the wise also.

EURYDIKE
Why do you insist on fair-sounding
words and tirades at my knees?
You've killed my child, Opheltes,
my eyes' joy. Take her inside
the palace so that before she dies,
she may ponder her guilt.

HYPSIPYLE
So, you plan to put me to death,
my lady, driven by anger,
without examining the events correctly?
You're silent? You say nothing? Ah,
wretched me.
I sigh not because I'll die,
although you wrongly think
that I could kill your child
whom I've raised in my arms,
loved dearly, fed, and
though I didn't give birth to him,
cared for as if he were my own, a true
joy to me!

Ah! Prow of Argo and foaming sea,
how unjustly I die. Oh, my children!

Amphiaraos enters.

Oh! seer, son of Oikleas,
come, help me! Otherwise, you'll see
me slain, condemned horribly.
I'm lost because of you. Come, you
know my case; this lady must welcome
you as my indisputable witness.
Come then, take me away! I see no
other friend to rescue me.
In vain I've shown piety.

Amphiaraos steps forward.

AMPHIARAOS
My queen, wait! Do not put this
woman to death! As I can see,
nobility and grace come naturally
to you.

Eurydike turns her back on Amphiaraos.
She remains unmoved.

HYPSIPYLE
Oh! Amphiaraos, I fall before your knees,
a suppliant, touching your beard
and honoring the seer's skill
given to you by Apollo! You come
at a critical moment of my misfortune.
Free me. You see me
bound, about to lose my life,
I, who helped you, strangers here.
Oh! You who with the prophecies
of fire foretell
the fate of the Greeks, explain to
this lady the doom that struck her
child. You were present and you
know; she believes
that I deliberately killed the precious boy.

AMPHIARAOS
I suspected what ills might have befallen you
because of the child's death and
I've come to help you in your suffering,
with piety only and not with force.
You've done much good to me.
And it would be horrible if I,
who have gained
so much from you, show no gratitude.
First, let me see your face, oh woman of Nemea.

Eurydike turns to face him.

The Greeks say that I have sound judgment,
oh woman, and by nature, I am well disciplined
and care only for what is right.
Listen to me! We must not act in haste.
We can err in many other things,
but when a woman's or a man's life
is at stake, then the evil is great.

EURYDIKE
Stranger, citizen of the land of Argos
that borders our land, I've heard from many people
that you are wise. I know this myself, though
I have never seen you before; now I wish
to hear from you and learn from you,
if you will, what is good; for you are honest.

AMPHIARAOS
If I lie to you, my witness is
Phoebos Apollo, whose art I practice
with oracular fires. I persuaded this woman
to show me a spring with pure water
in order to offer sacrifices to Zeus
so that the Argive passage through your land
and then to Thebes would be auspicious.

Out of piety she agreed,
and holding the child in her arms,
she led us to the spring; but
the child was crying, disturbing
the holy silence custom requires for sacrifices.
She put him on the grass and when
she had calmed him down,
she came back to us.
Then a snake from nearby,
frightened, shot forth and sped
straight for Opheltes
to wrap him in spirals of death.
Seeing this, we ran quickly
to rescue him. I shot my arrows
and killed the snake; but in vain;
your son was dead.

44

His death was for me
and for the Argives an omen:
the first death among so many others
destined to follow.
That is why I have named your child
Archemoros: the first death.
The beginning of doom for us,
because many of our soldiers will
die before the walls of Thebes,
and none of them will have
a homecoming. Of our seven
leaders only Adrastos will be saved
and return to Argos alone.
You know now what has happened.
Oh, woman, accept what I say:
No mortal is spared suffering;
he buries his children and gives birth to others,
until his turn comes to go to Hades.
This brings grief
to man. He becomes dust.
But we must reap life like an ear of wheat
heavy with seeds; one man lives
and another does not. Why should we
lament that which nature demands?
Nothing is more dreadful for people
than what is ordained.

And now,
let the Argives attend to their duty:
Allow us to bury your son.
Your mourning will not cease in a day;
mortal men will renew it and recall
your suffering forever.
I will found funeral games
in honor of your son's name,
and he will be famous throughout Greece.
I'll crown the glorious winners
with fresh wreaths in the very meadow
where your son, Opheltes, died.

EURYDIKE
In glory, my child, this worthy man
will bury you and the pain I feel
for your loss will be less.
One must consider circumstances
always according to the character
of men — bad or righteous — above all
according to the way they have lived their lives.
One must put one's faith in the wise,
never in the unjust.

I shall not put this woman to death; however,
when King Lykourgos returns,
I'll tell him everything, so that he may decide.

She signals to the guards to untie Hypsipyle's hands.

I enter the palace alone,
my dear boy to mourn.

AMPHIARAOS
Farewell Hypsipyle! I leave to prepare
the athletic games for Archemoros' funeral.
Fear no more for your life;
gods always hasten to help the good.
Take the bier and follow me.

They exit.

HYPSIPYLE
Farewell! You deserve a good fortune.

CHORUS
Your life is saved
thanks to the fair commander of the Argives.
Yet you seem anxious; what's wrong?
Will sorrow for the ill-fated child
not leave you?

HYPSIPYLE
I grieve for the unlucky baby.
And I feel that my suffering is not yet over.
You heard her words a while ago.
My life hangs from a single thread;
King Lykourgos will decide my fate.
If his wife was so harsh with me,
I fear the king will treat me
more cruelly; only
Amphiaraos could have saved me,
and he may come to help me again.
But you, whom I consider
a wise captain of a ship beaten
by the waves, tell me, what shall I do?

CHORUS
Let your mind think of no evil.
Fate will not always be adverse;
a god you've known has saved you.

HYPSIPYLE
What you say is true...It's Dionysos!
He's the root of my ancestors
and protects me and my sons,
if they're still alive; yes, they are, I know it;
I feel it deep in my heart.

CHORUS
Dionysos, horn-bearer,
son of Zeus, wandering
with your faithful dancers,
shouting at night in the mountains,
when the moon is shining in the sky,
lighting up the thick forests,
come, help her. She is Thoas'
daughter, of your own seed.
Free her and unite her
with her sons, lost for years.

As the god Dionysos slept
on the high-prowed ship, treacherous,
uncouth sailors drew near him;
but suddenly the mast was transformed
into a huge grapevine, sprouting
green leaves, red grapes;
drums were heard and the clattering
of krotala everywhere,
stern and prow,
and where the god had been,
a lion stood up roaring.

Terrified, the sailors
stepped back, but as their oars
turned into snakes,
they hurled themselves into the sea
to save themselves.
But you, O Lyaios Dionysos, set them free
from their human suffering.
You changed them into music-loving
dolphins, leaping in blue waters,
accompanying your vessel
to the beat of its music.

Fierce and entranced, O Dionysos,
you crossed over
to Egypt and Syria
and went to the peaks of Mount Tmolos,
so that the goddess Rhea could heal you;
and she, with purifications and magic spells,
taught you the secret rites
and the power of wild cries,
O Dionysos!

EURYDIKE

Coming out of the palace.

I go now to my son's burial.
I'll honor his fire of death
with new laments and funeral gifts.

To a mother who has lost her child
only tears are left.

CHORUS
You speak with reason, O Queen.
He'll be greatly honored by the Argives;
the seer has ensured him
great glory and a new name —
Archemoros — with an enduring life
in the minds of men.
He'll be our land's benevolent god.

EURYDIKE
Words of sympathy mean little to me
when my child lies dead,
making his last journey to the world below.
Bring the strangers here who asked
for hospitality at the palace.
I will welcome them despite my deep grief.
We must always honor the hospitality of Zeus.

CHORUS
Look! They're just coming out.

THOAS
We are here, Queen. You asked for us.

EURYDIKE
I'm told you are seeking hospitality.

THOAS
For this night only. But I see
you're dressed in mourning
and bearing funeral gifts.
I think this is not the proper time.

EURYDIKE
Mourning does not prevent me
from honoring the land's customs and laws:
philoxenia requires us always to
offer shelter to guests who need it.

This grief is mine. It's not proper
to impose it on other people's happiness.

THOAS
For your kindness, my queen,
may the gods repay you with equal grace.
Yet, I'd like to ask you something.

EURYDIKE
Please, do; and if I can, I'll answer you.

THOAS
You are dressed in mourning and your face is sad.
You hold funeral offerings. For whom?
A relative? A friend?

EURYDIKE
My son! My beloved, only son.

EUNEOS
Taken from you by illness?

EURYDIKE
A snake's venom put him to death.

THOAS
How did a snake get into the house?

EURYDIKE
It found my child alone in the meadow.

THOAS
How did your child get to the meadow?

EURYDIKE
A slave woman.

EUNEOS
What for? For what purpose?

EURYDIKE
She guided the army of the Argives
to a spring, and for a moment
she put the child down,
and the inevitable happened; the snake bit him.

THOAS
She offered to help the Argives
and misfortune struck.
A good act
turning bad.
How man's life and fate become
playthings in the gods' hands.

EURYDIKE
I go now. I must honor
my son's burial at the games.

EUNEOS
Will you not bury your child yourself?

EURYDIKE
The Argives will put him in his grave,
and renowned warriors will contend
around my son's altar,
celebrating his sudden death.
Amphiaraos asked me for this favor —
to bury my child and perform
athletic games at his burial,
respite for the grief
he brought upon me unwillingly.

THOAS
A great honor! A hero's burial!

EURYDIKE
Yet, my grief is no less.

THOAS
Unbearable is a mother's pain
losing her only child!

There is no respite!
My queen, let us ask a favor of you.

EURYDIKE
What favor, young strangers? Tell me.

THOAS
We wish to honor your son!
We'll compete at his burial fire
and if we win, we'll dedicate
our victory wreaths to him —
a small token for the kindness
you've shown us,
offering hospitality in unbearable grief.

EURYDIKE
Your request honors me.
The Argives select the contestants
and set the rules for the games.

THOAS
Then we ask you to
take us with you as your attendants
or as trusted friends, perhaps.
The Argives can't refuse to let us
compete with all the others.

EURYDIKE
You are right! There's a difficulty, though.

THOAS
What difficulty? Tell me.

EURYDIKE
All who will take part in the games —
the leaders, the great warriors of Argos —
are renowned men.
But no one knows you.

THOAS
We come from a royal root.
Dionysos, our protector and ancestor,
O Queen, is my witness to this truth.

EURYDIKE
Noble is your lineage, as your
faces and stature show.
I believe you; and above all,
I accept your wish to honor
my ill-fated child by taking part in the games.
You're noble, and the parents
who bore you and raised you so gallantly
must be very happy.

And you foolish slave,
stay in the palace, as long as I'm away.

Hypsipyle enters the palace.

Let us go, then; follow me.

They exit.

CHORUS
A woman's greatest joy
is to become a mother,
bear children,
raise them,
and see them grow.
Yet, she feels greater joy
when her children win
great fame,
doing splendid works
in virtue and valor
to benefit humankind.
Thus, I count
the fate of Alkmene
who gave birth
to illustrious Herakles,
and all people who revere her;

her son freed the world
from wild beasts,
monsters, illnesses, lawless acts;
he even came back from Hades alive;
when he died
he ascended to Olympos, among the gods.
But what grief and shame
when the unbearable pains
of childbirth bring forth
a godless, murderous, wrong-doing offspring.
May a woman so fated
never become a mother,
for she will pass her life
in total disgrace,
isolated, hearing everywhere
curses and insults
for her criminal children.

The greatest, the saddest
misery, though, falls upon a mother
when death snatches her children away
from her arms.
And this is three times worse,
when she's separated from her children,
without knowing whether she'll see them again;
then she weeps alone like a nightingale.
Hope alone consoles her,
a tiny spark in her heart,
that someday she'll find them again.
I think of all this —
Eurydike's and Hypsipyle's fate.
The queen had a child
taken suddenly down into Hades,
sinking her into grief.
Jason took Hypsipyle's two sons
as he sailed away on Argo to Kolchis.
Many years have passed since;
they never
saw their mother again.
If alive, they must be
in the prime of their youth.

An Argive soldier is approaching in a hurry!
What might he want? What news might he bring?

SECOND MESSENGER
Women of Nemea, where's that slave woman,
the nurse of that ill-fated child?
Call her, she must hear this.

CHORUS
Another disaster in the meadow?

SECOND MESSENGER
No! Good news! She must hear it.

CHORUS
Hypsipyle! Come out.

HYPSIPYLE

Appears.

What do you want, my dears? What's happening?

CHORUS
This man just came and has something
to tell you; you must hear it.

HYPSIPYLE
Are the rites and the games over?

SECOND MESSENGER
The last contest was starting
as I left. Amphiaraos, the seer,
sent me here to you.

HYPSIPYLE
What news do you bring me? I have known misfortune
for so many years now.

SECOND MESSENGER
All your suffering is over!

HYPSIPYLE
Are you speaking the truth, stranger, or do you mock me?

SECOND MESSENGER
Your children will be coming here soon.

HYPSIPYLE
This is beyond hope; I don't believe it.

SECOND MESSENGER
I tell the truth! Zeus is my witness.
You're no longer a slave; Queen Eurydike
granted you your freedom at the games,
before all the Argives.
Hear how all this happened.
First, they made sacrifices and slew oxen
on a stone altar, built
in the meadow where the baby died.
Then the seer, our leader,
prayed to Zeus and the gods
to grant a fair journey to our army
and that Opheltes' death may be
a good omen for us. He said all this
with tearful eyes and a sad face.
Then, soldiers piled up branches beneath
the infant's bier and lit them;
when the flames died out,
Amphiaraos gathered the ashes
in a small golden jar and gave them
to his mother, Queen Eurydike.

When all this had ended,
the Argives gathered at the meadow's edge.
The herald appeared in the center,
dressed in black, and with a loud voice
proclaimed the games; those who wished
could compete in honor of Archemoros.
They marked the track, and the games began.
The prize for each victor would be a wreath
of wild celery, and Adrastos himself, the king
of Argos, would crown him.

56

The first contest was boxing,
and Tydeus won the victory.
Polyneikes came first in free wrestling.
Parthenopaios was decided by all
to be the best archer — he didn't miss
his target even once.
Eteoklos won the discus,
and Hippomedon, the javelin.
When the herald announced those who would
compete in the foot races,
the two young men who had come with Queen Eurydike
presented themselves among others.
Amphiaraos saw them, called them to come near,
and asked them: "Who are you, strangers?
You don't seem to be Argive warriers;
your garments, however, show that you are Greeks.
Why have you come here to compete?"
They said: "We honor the queen's grief,
who graciously offered us hospitality."
Eurydike was standing beside them.
"That's why we ask to compete,
to show our gratitude to her."
He asked again: "Of what lineage?"
They answered: "We proudly say
that Jason is our father and Hypsipyle,
Queen of Lemnos, our mother.
Our forefather is the great Dionysos."
He was amazed
and asked them: "What token do you have
that truly proves your lineage?
What are your names?"
"My name is Thoas," replied one,
"and this is Euneos."
He took a golden necklace from his neck,
showed it, and said:
"Here is the blossom of our ancestral god,
the holy sacred vine; he had given it as a token
to the son he had with Ariadne."
That's how your two sons competed
in the race alongside the Argives.
When the signal was given, they dashed forth

like a swift wind, surpassing quickly
all the others, and finished first,
stepping on the finish line together.
The meadow resounded from end to end
with shouting from the crowd, and all hailed
the two strangers. Then,
crowned with their wreaths, they went
to the grave where Queen Euridyke stood,
and there they laid the wreaths of their victories.
All the land resounded
again with loud cries and new praise,
and all blessed the mother of the two youths.
Then Amphiaraos turned toward
the Queen and told her this:
"Queen, these valiant youths to whom you offered
hospitality, have honored your son's grave
to the highest degree. You must reward them,
and let them join their mother,
whom they seek so passionately.
You know who I mean,
the slave woman, the nurse
you have in your home.
Free her, she is of noble lineage.
Slavery doesn't become her.
Know this, too: the gods wish it as well. Listen to me."
She stood pensively for a while
and then, looking straight at him, she said:
"You're a wise man and a seer, Amphiaraos,
and through the darkness of time, you see
what will happen in the future. I do not
wish to disobey the will of the gods.
I free her now; send someone
to bring the news to Hypsipyle."
And straight away, I was ordered
to bring the news of joy, and the message
that soon he'll arrive with your sons.
And as I see this change of your fortune,
I think that nothing happens to mortals by chance.
They must keep their hopes alive for all things.
For the gods always look after their people.

He exits.

HYPSIPYLE
My dears, I can't believe this;
I find my sons and I gain my freedom!
I can't believe it! It is unreal.

CHORUS
You've just heard it; it's true.

HYPSIPYLE
Oh! I thank you, great gods.
You offered me three gifts,
and I don't know which is the best.
My life was hanging by a thread,
and you've saved me. I am free.
And my sons, lost for years,
alive only in my most secret hopes,
will come here and I'll hold them in my arms.
This is something more than a miracle.
My heart swells with joy,
and the sweet song rises from within me.

CHORUS
You were the most unhappy of women,
and now you surpass in happiness
all other women. Stricken terribly
by misfortune and pain
you find your sons unexpectedly! They'll be here soon.

HYPSIPYLE
Beloved friends, sing a paean,
praising the gods who helped me!
To them and Fortune I owe everything.

CHORUS
Oh! Fortune, daughter
of Okeanos, blind goddess,
interweaving the deeds
of mortals as you like,
now you raise them

to happiness and now
you plunge them into misery.
Accept this song
of thanks graciously.
We'll honor you
with circle dances,
beating with force our feet to the earth.
I pray you, keep my life
always at the wheel's peak;
let me delight myself
in all her joys
and never let me fall below,
where tears, suffering
and sadness abound.
A song of praise
I sing to Bacchus, too —
ancestral god of your family.
He made Fortune
entwine like threads
the actions of mortals
so that all
would end happily.

HYPSIPYLE
They're late; they won't come; it was a lie.

CHORUS
When one's in a hurry, time moves slowly.
It doesn't follow our heartbeat.

HYPSIPYLE
I see no one — no one coming here
on the path through the meadow.

CHORUS
You're impatient.
Look! Now you can see people approaching.

AMPHIARAOS

Enters with Hypsipyle's sons.

Hail, Hypsipyle. Your many sufferings
are over. Queen Eurydike
sets you free; you're no longer a slave.
These valiant lads beside me
seek their lost mother,
and you, I think, your lost sons.
What you seek — is before you.

HYPSIPYLE
Ah! What can I say?
May the gods always bless you
and help you, Amphiaraos,
if what I see is true,
and my longing doesn't deceive me.

AMPHIARAOS
These are your sons; don't you recognize them?

HYPSIPYLE
They were still babies when they took them from me.
What resemblance could there be between these men
and those little boys? All things change.
But there's a sign,
untouched by time's passing.
Before your father took you away,
your mother put an ornament around the neck of one of you,
a sign of the origin of our ancestry.

EUNEOS
You mean this, the vine!

HYPSIPYLE
Oh, yes! Dionysos' sacred plant!
You must be Thoas, then.

EUNEOS
And I am Euneos, speaking to you.

HYPSIPYLE
My beloved, come to my arms,
small babies then,

valiant lads now,
my pride and honor!
Hope has not deceived me.
I was denied the chance to raise you as your mother;
you grew up away from me.
But deprivation and grief are forgotten now!
I hold you tightly in my arms —
mine forever.

EUNEOS
Beloved mother, you are
an unexpected gift from the gods to us.
We thought you were lost forever,
but the caring gods helped
Fortune reunite us.
When we were in Pageon, the land
of Edonon, we never believed
we'd find you again;
but now we
hold you in our arms.

CHORUS
Wheel of Fortune
into the same path again
mother and children reunites.
She led them in oblique ways
through misery and happiness,
but now with time's passing
the happiest day has come.

AMPHIARAOS
The favor you did for me, oh Lady,
courageously helping me when I was
in need, to you and your children
I heartily repay.
Take care of yourself. And you, my lads,
protect your mother. Farewell!
We must press forward, leading
the army to Thebes.

THOAS
Farewell, friend; you are a worthy man.

EUNEOS
Farewell!
But what implacable god
was the cause of so much misery
for you, Mother?

HYPSIPYLE
My child! Hear about my secret escape
through the foamy sea of Lemnos,
because I could not bear to slay my father.

EUNEOS
They ordered you to kill your father?

HYPSIPYLE
For those horrid deeds, fear
still seizes me; like gorgons,
oh, my children, they killed
their husbands in their beds.

EUNEOS
But how were you saved from death?

HYPSIPYLE
I went down to the roaring sea
and, in an empty osprey's nest,
pushed off into the waves.

EUNEOS
How did you come here?

HYPSIPYLE
Seamen found me and brought me by ship
to Nauplia's harbor, my child,
where they sold me, wretched me! A slave
here, in the land of Nemea.

EUNEOS
Ah! What misery.

HYPSIPYLE
When we're happy, we must not complain.
But who raised you and your brother,
my valiant lad, my child?
Tell your mother, tell your story.

EUNEOS
Argo brought us to Kolchis.

HYPSIPYLE
Still babies, they took you from my arms.

EUNEOS
When Jason, my father disappeared...

HYPSIPYLE
Ah! What disaster! You fill
my eyes with tears, child.

EUNEOS
Orpheus led us to Thrace.

HYPSIPYLE
Doing a favor for your unlucky father?
Tell me, my child.

EUNEOS
Orpheus taught me to play Asian music
with my lyre; and my brother
learned the art of weapons and of war.

HYPSIPYLE
By what ship did you reach the coast of Lemnos,
crossing the Aegean Sea?

EUNEOS
Thoas, your father, took us there.

HYPSIPYLE
Truly? Is he saved? Is he alive?

EUNEOS
With Dionysos' care.

HYPSIPYLE
How swiftly everything changes.
Dark miseries vanish and Thoas,
who had few hopes to live,
returned to Lemnos with his two grandsons
and sent them away to find their mother.
But tell me, why hasn't he
come himself to search for his daughter
who saved him from the darkness of death?

THOAS
He's grown old. Years
and miseries lie heavily upon him
as he tries hard to bring law and order
to the island; he's anxiously waiting
for us to return to him.

HYPSIPYLE
And from Jason, your lost father, you bring me
no sign, nothing?

EUNEOS
Nothing; except a token he left with Orpheus,
to pass on to us.

HYPSIPYLE
What is it? Do you have it with you?

EUNEOS
A piece from the Golden Fleece of Kolchis
with your name written on the back.
It's with our things, inside the palace.

HYPSIPYLE
Bring me the token; let me see it.

The two youths enter the palace.

To the chorus:

My dears, I can't restrain
the happiness overwhelming me!
These valiant youths are mine
and Jason's offspring.
They'll bring me what is, perhaps, his last message.
Ah! Unbroken is our truth and my joy.

CHORUS
You shouldn't doubt that!

HYPSIPYLE
No, I don't doubt; yet there's no harm
in seeking a stronger assurance.

CHORUS
Someone's coming; it's King Lykourgos.

Lykourgos enters with his attendants.

LYKOURGOS
Where's the slave woman who wrought such
havoc upon my home?

HYPSIPYLE
You are looking for me... I'm no longer a slave.

LYKOURGOS
Who set you free without my knowing?

HYPSIPYLE
Your wife, Queen Eurydike.

LYKOURGOS
As a reward for killing my son!

HYPSIPYLE
I am not to be blamed. It is the work of fate alone.

68

LYKOURGOS
You blame fate for abandoning
a baby, leaving it alone and unprotected?
Who taught you that?

HYPSIPYLE
No one. I had to help Amphiaraos...

LYKOURGOS
Amphiaraos? That seer of evil, who has slain
my father Pronakta?
You helped my greatest enemy?
Now I understand the plot. Evil ones
always think that profit is more powerful than justice.

HYPSIPYLE
I did nothing for profit; I led him
to the spring to get water for a sacrifice,
when a snake killed Opheltes.

LYKOURGOS
I've heard that; the cunning seer
with treacherous words and promises
deceived Euridyke,
but she sent me a message and I've come in time.

I think you're getting ready to leave,
without paying for my child's death;
but the gods are never fond of evil.
That's why I've come, to punish you, as you deserve.

HYPSIPYLE
My children, Thoas and Euneos, hurry,
save your mother.

LYKOURGOS
You can't be saved by lost sons.

HYPSIPYLE
They're here! You'll see them now before you.
Hurry, my children, come out of the palace.

LYKOURGOS
You speak the truth, perhaps. Attendants,
go to the door and guard it with swords in hand.
Let no one come out, until I've
punished this woman, as she deserves.

HYPSIPYLE
Gods, I implore you, help me!

LYKOURGOS
Gods do not assist murderers.
You killed my son! You'll die
yourself, ungrateful woman, by my own hand,
and no fate can save you now.

DIONYSOS

Appearing on the Theologeion.

Hold back your anger, Lykourgos,
and don't commit such an impious act.
I speak to you, I, Dionysos.
This woman is of my seed;
she's not to blame for your son's death.
The wrongdoer is you, who disobeyed

Apollo's oracle that said:
"Before the infant can stand alone
on its own feet and walk, until then,
do not let him touch the earth
without a guard beside him;
or else he will go down to Hades."

That's why all this had to happen:
this woman
broke an oath
and was punished bitterly.
She has found her happiness again.
By breaking her oath then,
she saved her father and did not
defile my lineage with his murder.
Let Hypsipyle return
to Lemnos and be rewarded for what she has done.

You've lost your son, and you are in mourning.
However, his death will bring glory
and pride to Nemea; he'll be a
god for this land, your protector forever,
and his name will be Archemoros — "the first death."
You'll offer sacrifices to him, and every third year
athletic games will take place in this land,
where the bravest men will gather
from all over Greece.
Hold no enmity against Amphiaraos.
He has not killed, as it is rumored,
your father, Pronakta. He had no part
whatsoever in his murder. You should not
hate him — a short life only is left to him
once he reaches the gates of Thebes.

And you, Hypsipyle, with one of your sons,
Thoas, I mean, go to Lemnos
and live your life happily.
Euneos will go to Kekrops' land, to Athens,
and his lineage will become renowned
for music of the lyre
for countless years to come.

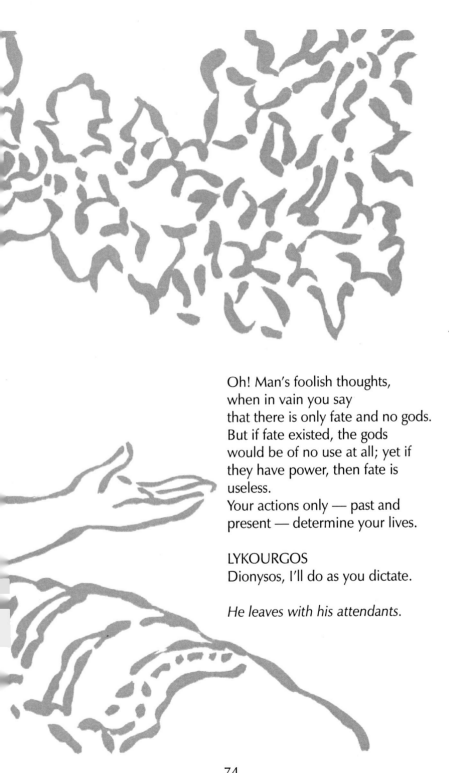

Oh! Man's foolish thoughts,
when in vain you say
that there is only fate and no gods.
But if fate existed, the gods
would be of no use at all; yet if
they have power, then fate is
useless.
Your actions only — past and
present — determine your lives.

LYKOURGOS
Dionysos, I'll do as you dictate.

He leaves with his attendants.

HYPSIPYLE
I thank you, father of my race.
I'll follow your commands faithfully.

Dionysos disappears from the theologeion.

CHORUS
Events shaped by gods take many forms,
and the gods may end them, unexpectedly.
What we think we foresee does not happen.
The gods find a way for the unforeseen.
And so, this drama has come to an end.

"The cover image is my interpretation of a section of an ancient vase painting. I etched the image on a copper plate, but left out lines to suggest the fragmentary state of the play itself before its reconstruction. The ink drawings are based on ancient vase paintings depicting the story of *Hypsipyle*. I drew selected scenes and characters relating to the major events of the play.

In adaptations for the book, photographs from the dramatic reading of the play produced by The Greek Institute on December 3, 2001 at the Stuart Street Playhouse in Boston, appear superimposed on each image. Then the modern and ancient worlds and the world of gods and men appear in tandem."

- *Catherine Kernan*

"Euripides' *Hypsipyle* belongs to his lost tragedies. It is rooted in the mythological material of the Theban plays and was taught in approximately 408BCE in Athens, along with the *Phoenikes* and *Antiope*. Aristophanes refers to it in *The Frogs*... I was encouraged to complete the play because the story of the play and many details of the plot were known. I was also aided by many scholars, and especially by the exceptional study of G.W. Bond, *Euripides' Hypsipyle*, Oxford, 1963... The completion of a lost tragedy, although supported by one's knowledge of the style and technique of the poet, remains a romantic illusion."

- *Tasos Roussos*

All photographs are by Nina Nickles.